The Great Training Robbery

MANAGEMENT POCKETBOOKS

The Great Training Robbery

By **John Townsend**
(Master Trainer Institute)

and **Paul Donovan**
(Irish Management Institute)

Drawings by Phil Hailstone

With thanks to our models: Charles Bishop - *Manager*

Debby Moss - *Trainer*

John Mears - *Judge*

© **John Townsend 2001**
Paul Donovan 2001

Published by: Management Pocketbooks Ltd
14 East Street, Alresford, Hants SO24 9EE
Tel: +44 (0)1962 735573 Fax: +44 (0)1962 733637
E-mail: sales@pocketbook.co.uk
www.pocketbook.co.uk

This edition published 2001

ISBN 1 870471 88 1

Designed and typeset by: artsFX Ltd, Eastleigh, Hants

Printed in U.K. by: Ashford Colour Press Ltd, Gosport, Hants

INTRODUCTION

Over the years we have been frustrated, as trainers, that companies and organisations have regarded training as a second class function. They have robbed training of its potential impact on company results by treating courses as recreational restoration, or necessary comic relief, or as a safety valve for organisational tensions.

In order to examine whether or not our frustrations are justified, we have decided to put management on trial.

This book is an allegory in the form of The Great Training Robbery.
It describes:

- The Robbery, in a series of newspaper articles
- The Trial, with training as prosecution and management as defence
- The Verdict, which finds training guilty of shooting itself in the foot or of perpetrating an inside job
- The Sentence, which comprises the steps that training needs to take to get the money back

INTRODUCTION

The Story So Far …

You are about to read newspaper reports of The Great Training Robbery. As economies prosper and as management pays lip service to training, the millions invested have been wasted because companies are organising courses that have no impact. Throughout the world, reports are flooding in of trainers accusing their companies of the theft of training resources and influence.

This is The Great Training Robbery! Now read on.

CHAPTER 1

THE ROBBERY

When Wall Street Sneezes, Training Catches Cold!

THE DEPRESSING news from this year's Worldwide Training Conference is that as soon as economic indices dip, trainers all over the world find their budgets being cut.

"When the shares are down," said one disgruntled Canadian training manager, "when the company needs us most to help streamline processes and update skills - that's when they strip our resources!"

"It used to be advertising," says a young trainer from Holland, "but now it's training that's the first to be cut. I feel I've got my finger in the dyke and it's management trying to pull it out. I just can't stop the company sinking single-handed."

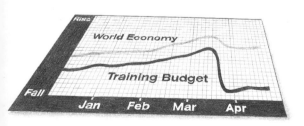

Management Insist on À La Carte Training

A MAJOR MULTINATIONAL was recently accused by its training department of using a menu approach to training. This wasteful method apparently allows employees to choose what they want rather than what they need. No formal training needs analysis is asked for.

As a result, many people are choosing subjects that they like instead of learning something useful for their jobs.

The training staff accuse management of robbing the organisation of a good solution by insisting on a menu approach to training courses. This is not geared to solving business problems or capitalising on business opportunities.

Company Shoots Itself in the Foot

RUMOURS are rife of squandered resources in a large European computer manufacturer. The company invested in front-line management training for its team leaders.

Following a brilliantly executed training programme, the team leaders, on their end-of-course forms, evaluated the offering as being excellent.

However, on return to the workplace they became frustrated because the company did nothing to encourage them to use their new skills.

Trainers accuse the company of wasting a lot of money because its leaders couldn't be bothered to think through what management culture they really wanted.

A TRAINING SCANDAL has come to light. A medium-sized public sector body conducted a highly-rated programme for its front line staff. Sources close to the organisation say that trainers were appalled at the lack of results achieved from the programme and so they set up an evaluation exercise in the form of an investigation.

This investigation showed that the operators already had the knowledge, the skills and the right attitudes required **before** they went on the training course. Their poor performance had been due to low morale as a result of poor management style. The training department complained that the organisation's investment was frittered away.

Preaching to the Converted

INTERNAL INVESTIGATION

Swiss Managers Cheesed Off!

TRAINING proves to be counter-productive!

Trainers in a medium-sized finance company in Lausanne were bemused by the results of a recent costly training programme. Following the management skills programme, end-of-course feedback forms reported overwhelming demotivation.

The only result of the training seems to have been that the participants were frustrated that their bosses used none of the management practices that they themselves had just learned!

Great Training .... Where's the Door?

CAN TRAINING help you get a better job?

It certainly did for 50% of the operators at a north of England auto parts manufacturer. As a result of a highly popular, well-designed and pacy training programme for the shop-floor staff on how to use new technology, half of them have handed in their notice!

"It's not really disloyalty," says one frustrated operator, "but the company's IT systems just aren't in line with what we were taught. There are other employers crying out for our skills."

Outward Bound to Fail

A MAJOR US corporation based in Brussels recently conducted a 6-month follow-up on an outward bound survival type training programme for its top management. During the programme, the course tutors had expressed amazement at how well office-based executives could cope with the adversity of a hostile outdoor environment.

The organisers of the training were delighted with 'off-the-scale' feedback ratings. However, a 360° evaluation conducted six months after the training revealed an actual decrease of 15.6% in team members' satisfaction with their bosses' management style.

THE TRAINING MANAGER of a US multinational with branches in most of the Emirates in the Gulf is up in arms following a recent supervisory skills workshop for the company's local managers.

The workshop covered areas like empowerment and communications. It seems that the only tangible result of the training was that the CEO has had a special back door built in his office so that he can come straight in from his parked Rolls Royce at 10.30 am, rather than walk through the office area and be confronted with direct reports trying to communicate with him!

Gulf Grows Between CEO and Managers

Walk the Talk Backlash Strikes French Firm

A LARGE French organisation is experiencing an embarrassing sequel to a recent training seminar, designed to inspire employees with the company's newly introduced 'vision and values' statement.

The company, whose mission includes *we believe in treating all of our stakeholders with respect* and puts emphasis on behaviour to encourage values like *trust, entrepreneurship* and *teamwork,* is facing growing criticism from staff who have completed the training.

"Management just doesn't walk the talk," they say, and the workforce at one of their plants in Normandy is planning a one-day strike next week, to protest against *archaic and discriminatory management practices.*

When contacted by phone, the training manager refused to comment.

Calculator Company Counts the Cost

A HIGH TECH instruments company in the US is today assessing the damage done to its employee relations' climate following a review of a major management development programme. On the surface, the training needs analysis seemed to have been done well, establishing the exact requirements of management to meet the needs of the organisation's long-term business strategy. The programme had been well put together and the participants reported that the programme successfully achieved its aims and objectives.

Unfortunately, the programme review exercise undertaken six months later shows almost no change in the performance of the managers who attended the programme. One manager informally commented that it was a great course, but he hadn't had time to put any of it into practice. Another manager suggested that she wouldn't dare try some of those techniques with her current manager.

Management was unavailable for comment.

Italian Trainers Pasta their Best?

THE GIANT electrical components manufacturer Lampa last night hit out at poor training results achieved following huge investment in a major skills development programme, conducted by one of Italy's leading training organisations.

The training company's representatives reacted angrily to the news, suggesting that the mercenary reward system operated by the manufacturer almost guaranteed that the trainees would not change their behaviour following the training. One irate trainer was quoted as saying that 'although the training was all about giving the participants better teamworking skills, the company's reward system encourages individual effort and effectively punishes staff when they collaborate with each other'. Another trainer suggested that the company was rewarding one thing and hoping for another.

The two sides are likely to meet next week to discuss the situation.

CHAPTER 2

THE TRIAL

The Trial

Management is on trial for robbing training of its impact, influence and effectiveness by not believing in people development. Frustrated training managers all over the world have been complaining for years that companies simply don't want to invest seriously in training their employees. Trainers accuse leaders of paying lip service to training but neglecting to integrate it into the organisation's strategic thinking.

The trial has been one of the longest running in the history of organisational development. This chapter presents the charges against management, and a synopsis of the arguments for the prosecution (Training), and the defence (Management), in the form of a hypothetical courtroom dialogue between the two parties.

The judge's verdict will be presented in Chapter 3.

The Charges

Management is charged as follows:

1 Wasting time and money by selfishly demanding training courses to assuage their guilt about paying insufficient attention to human resource development. Random triggers such as television programmes or peer pressure often prompt these events.

2 Diverting the thrust of the training effort by insisting that training courses are provided that reflect what *they* enjoyed in the past instead of what the organisation needs now.

3 Resisting new ideas by refusing to support innovative and creative initiatives in training and development.

4 Being seduced by silver-tongued devils rather than investing in solid training facilitators.

5 Treating training courses as a reward rather than as a development necessity.

6 Equating trainer effectiveness with scores on the 'happy sheet' rather than workplace outcomes.

7 Adopting a 'check the box' approach to nominating trainees for courses.

8 Using training as a quick-fix remedy rather than as a strategic solution.

LEADERSHIP GUILT OR SETTING DIRECTION?

Charge Number 1

> **W**asting time and money by selfishly demanding training courses to assuage their guilt about paying insufficient attention to human resource development. Random triggers such as television programmes or peer pressure often prompt these events.

Training says:

Periodically, leaders will see a TV programme, go to a conference or speak to a colleague and start to feel guilty about not doing enough training in their organisations. Their hearts are in the right place but this kind of guilt-driven training simply provides a flurry of unconnected training events, unplanned and unmeasured, which cause us more problems than they solve. We are left with all the patching-up work caused by lack of objectives and no follow-up.

Management says:

Of course we feel guilty! We'd really love to spend more money on training - if we could see the benefit! When we come to you with ideas for training which have been triggered from outside the organisation, **YOU** should feel guilty. It's **YOUR** job to provide us with the information, the updates, the prompting to help us decide what the best training would be. **YOU** should be providing input on training objectives and on systems for measuring success.

TRAINING AS FUN OR PERSONAL DEVELOPMENT?

Charge Number 2

66 Diverting the thrust of the training effort by insisting that training courses are provided that reflect what they enjoyed in the past instead of what the organisation needs now. 99

Training says:

Many managers have learned at least one catch-phrase from the training they received: 'You gotta look after your people,' or something similar. Unfortunately, this often means that they ask us to do the right thing and get some training courses organised, whether or not there's any real business issue behind them. They want things like Time Management or Communication Skills. Now, these areas are important but they are sometimes a bit fluffy. All that managers seem to care about is that their teams enjoy themselves. They **never** ask us to evaluate whether they were effective in changing behaviour and helping the business.

Management says:

Yes, we do believe that you've got to look after your people ... but we're not experts on training. So we make mistakes.

OK, so we get enthusiastic about certain types of training like Time Management. That's because we enjoyed those kinds of courses so much when you put them on for us! Have you ever thought of saying 'no' to us when we get the wrong end of the stick? Why are you so scared of being professional? We'd really like you to help us measure the effectiveness of training like this.

What do you suggest?

REJECTING NEW THINKING OR KEEPING UP WITH TRENDS?

Charge Number 3

" Resisting new ideas by refusing to support innovative and creative initiatives in training and development. "

Training says:

One of our jobs is to keep up to date with new trends in training. We think it's very important for our organisations to have a modern outlook and provide their employees with the latest developments. We feel really frustrated when management takes a 'dinosaur' approach and insists that the old ways are the best.

Management says:

It's true, we're not always convinced that 'flavour of the month' training brings results. We sometimes feel that you trainers just want to jump on the bandwagon of some new fad before any link can be proven to improving company success.

What we'd like you to do is to help us look at our strategy and see if the new trend is going to affect us. Then we'd like you to do some benchmarking to see how other organisations have benefited from this kind of training. Lastly, we could look at specific needs and tailor the training to help those who can really use it.

'ENTERTRAINING' OR SERIOUS LEARNING?

Charge Number 4

> " Being seduced by silver-tongued
> devils rather than investing in solid
> training facilitators. "

Training says:

Although we agree that training should be fun and motivating, we hate to see our budgets wasted on evangelistic style presentation events and courses, which management wants organised at holiday resorts or near golf courses. This is tough for us because, as professionals, we know that the transfer of learning after these events is virtually zero while the feedback from participants is nearly always fantastic ... so we get a good reputation for doing bad training!

Management says:

Guilty, m'lud! But only if it's a crime to give our teams a good time occasionally! Surely it's important to take the opportunity to motivate the troops and try to teach them something at the same time. Even if you killjoy trainers would rather have us shut into some seedy seminar room in Slough!

TRAINING AS PERK OR PERSONAL DEVELOPMENT?

Charge Number 5

> " Treating training courses as a reward
> rather than as a development necessity. "

Training says:

Training should be designed to help people develop their skills, knowledge and attitudes so that they can do present or future jobs better and help the organisation meet its objectives. Too often, management sees training as a perk or reward after successful projects - a way of thanking people for good performance, whether or not they need it. Training time is therefore seen as vacation time.

It's very embarrassing for us to hear trainees' managers welcoming them back from our courses with, 'Well, how were the holidays then? Ready to get back to work in the real world?'.

Management says:

Mmmm! Well, that's certainly the way many of us got our training, and we did learn something. You know, busy people just can't afford time away from their jobs at the drop of a hat, and sometimes we can only spare them at certain times of the year. Surely it's the good ones you want to develop (OK, reward) so they can move up in the organisation?

'HAPPY SHEET' MYOPIA OR ON THE JOB RESULTS?

Charge Number 6

" Equating trainer effectiveness with scores on the 'happy sheet' rather than workplace outcomes. "

Training says:

There is no proven link between how much people enjoy training and how much they learn and change as a result of it. Unfortunately, management thinks that good trainers and good training can be judged from 'happy sheets' filled in after each course.

Many of us resent the lack of professionalism of this because it favours trainers who 'play to the gallery'. We all know how easy it is to influence participants to give us good ratings, and it doesn't have a lot to do with stretching them with new skills and forcing them out of their comfort zone!

Management says:

Now wait a minute! You're pushing your luck on this one! We need to be able to evaluate you trainers. You're an expensive service to our organisation. How else can we know whether you're doing a good job? These forms we ask you for are a great measure of success. They tell us whether your customers are happy with your products. And we all know that happy customers stay with us!

BUMS ON SEATS OR SKILLS IMPROVEMENT?

Charge Number 7

" Adopting a 'check the box' approach
to nominating trainees for courses. "

Training says:

I t seems to us that management treats training like an administrative chore. We hear things like, 'Everyone's supposed to get their one week's training per year. Put my people down for the usual. Here's the timing schedule.' They don't seem to have any expectations of skills improvement. They never give us any feedback. It's like they're checking off boxes.

Management says:

T o be honest, your approach to training is so bureaucratic and institutional that we've got into the habit of treating it like a necessary evil. We have pretty low expectations so anything is better than nothing! There's nothing to get excited about.

31

KNEE-JERK RESPONSES OR STRATEGIC APPROACH?

Charge Number 8

" Using training as a quick-fix remedy
rather than as a strategic solution. "

Training says:

Very often managers ask us to organise training events at very short notice as a result of some crisis or other. Not only are these requests very difficult to handle, but the objectives are often unclear and the manager's idea of course content rather woolly, to say the least.

'We need some communications skills training, and fast!'

'Get some training for my front office people, we're losing customers!'

The big problem is that there's no strategic thinking behind these requests and no attempt is made to measure success. These are just knee-jerk reactions to crises.

Management says:

Well, why not? That's what training is for, isn't it? Improving performance. We can't sit around and wait for you to come up with your catalogue, which may or may not include useful training courses for our people. Training should be aimed at solving day to day performance problems.

If you want strategically planned training which we can measure, then come and sit down with us more often. If you really push us, we might even give you some ideas for course content – we might even train on some of them ourselves!

CHAPTER 3

THE VERDICT

The judge has deliberated on these serious charges
and gives the following judgment.

Charge Number 1

Wasting time and money by selfishly demanding training courses to assuage their guilt about paying insufficient attention to human resource development. Random triggers such as television programmes or peer pressure often prompt these events.

Training's arguments seem to focus on management being impetuous and demanding courses as a reaction to feeling guilty about not doing enough for the development of people in the organisation. Management should instead be concentrating on courses that help set direction and provide consistent leadership.

Management responds by stating that these 'spontaneous' actions, triggered from *outside* the organisation, are taken to fill the void created by the lack of prompting from *inside* the organisation by the training department.

*On balance, I agree with **management**. I feel it is the role of training to be, as it were, management's conscience and to be proactive in proposing training initiatives.*

I therefore find management not guilty under this charge.

Instead, I find training guilty of failing to offer sufficient advice and new initiatives.

My verdict is that training is guilty of failing to provide management with timely information on new ideas, and guilty of neglecting to propose useful training objectives and solutions.

Charge Number 2

Diverting the thrust of the training effort by insisting that training courses are provided that reflect what they enjoyed in the past instead of what the organisation needs now.

My understanding of training's arguments is that managers think everyone will enjoy what they enjoyed and that enjoyment is important, whether or not the training is effective.

Management admits to some guilt in this area but accuses training of allowing them to get away with it.

Thinking back to my own legal training, I can only agree with management that it is natural to want for others what you enjoyed yourself. In fact I find this quite a noble sentiment. However, the whims of managers (and judges) must be countered by rigorous training needs analysis. For example, I would expect the Law Society's Education Committee, as the responsible body entrusted with identifying the training needs of the profession, to determine what is appropriate for my colleagues and me to learn.

I therefore declare management not guilty under this charge.

Training, however, I find guilty of failing to follow through their needs analysis findings and even, sometimes, failing to conduct training needs analysis at all!

Resisting new ideas by refusing
to support innovative and
creative initiatives in training
and development.

Training accuses managers of being dinosaurs who resist new trends.

Management accuses trainers of adopting a 'flavour of the month' approach.

I feel obliged to rule in favour of management, in that fads are usually repackaging of old material. Take the management topic of worker motivation, for example. My researchers have shown me that this first emerged as Initiative in Henri Fayol's early work around 1910. The subject re-emerged as Human Relations in the Hawthorne Experiments of the 1930s. Maslow's work in 1945 on the Hierarchy of Needs was followed by Herzberg's Hygiene Factors in the 1960s. Genie Laborde called it Dovetailing in the 1980s and Tom Peters contributed to the idea of Empowerment that was all the rage in the 1990s.

Goodness knows what the next repackaging will be as we move into this new century!

Yes, under this charge I find many trainers guilty of taking a 'flavour of the month' approach.

Being seduced by silver-tongued devils rather than investing in solid training facilitators.

T rainers decry the cosmetically attractive packaging of some 'evangelical' style training events. They claim that learning transfer is virtually non-existent.

M anagement responds, 'guilty, m'lud' but only to having philanthropic tendencies towards their staff. They argue that important learning doesn't have to be painful or be delivered in boring surroundings by tedious trainers.

I myself am partial to an entertaining speaker. On many occasions I have seen a jury being entertained by an animated prosecution or defence attorney. However, I truly believe that people are not stupid and that if they are swayed it is for very good reasons.

I therefore find management not guilty under this charge.

In fact, I would like trainers to prove their claim that people don't learn anything from these events and I suspend judgment until they can!

Charge Number 5

Treating training courses as a reward rather than as a development necessity.

Trainers say that managers view training as a reward for good work and a well-deserved break after a successful project.

Management responds that there is too much work pressure and that they can't spare good people for training.

On this charge, I find in favour of training.

I am told by my researchers that current training will always lower current productivity. I think that managers must take this lowering of efficiency as the necessary price to pay for future results.

Managers are, therefore, guilty as charged.

Charge Number 6

Equating trainer effectiveness with scores on the 'happy sheet' rather than workplace outcomes.

Trainers resent being measured according to forms filled in at the end of courses. They argue that management is measuring enjoyment rather than learning.

Management contends that 'happy sheets' measure customer satisfaction which, to them, is paramount.

I find reaction evaluation forms a necessary but not sufficient method of measuring the effectiveness of training courses. My research leads me to agree with trainers that there is no link between positive reaction evaluation results and learning gained by participants.

However, I understand management's arguments that the customer's (participant's) satisfaction is important.

My decision, therefore, is to rule against both training and management because both seem to have missed the real issue which is to manage the 'transfer environment'. My sentence will explain further my thinking on this matter.

Adopting a 'check the box' approach to nominating trainees for courses.

Trainers argue that some managers take a bureaucratic and uninterested approach to sending staff on training courses.

Management defends this attitude by accusing trainers of providing unexciting and ineffective offerings.

*Thinking back to my own training and to the programmes offered to my legal team, **I have to find managers not guilty under this charge**. If, as I suspect, their world is like our world, then the annual training plan can easily become a 'check the box' affair.*

I therefore find training guilty under this charge in that the all too common menu-driven structure of training offerings can only encourage a limited and often mechanistic response from management.

Using training as a quick-fix remedy rather than as a strategic solution.

Trainers accuse managers of being too reactive and impetuous in their training demands.

Management, faced with day to day crises, claims that training should be aimed at short-term performance improvement.

I am inclined to distinguish between training and development. Day to day changes in the workplace often require rapid changes in the knowledge, skills and attitudes of staff. These requirements must be addressed by training. Development, however, should be viewed as a more long-term change that prepares people to take on greater responsibility whatever the changes in the day to day environment.

Although I understand trainers' frustration at having to organise what they describe as 'knee-jerk' response training events, I have to admit that our fast-moving world requires an equally fast-moving approach to training.

I therefore find management not guilty under this charge. Human performance improvement must be tied to day to day problems as well as future development.

Training, on the other hand, I find guilty of failing to distinguish properly between training (short-term) and development (long-term) and of neglecting to include top management in their strategic design and delivery process (if they have one!).

Summing Up

Although management stands accused on eight charges of robbing training of its impact and not believing in people development, I have found trainers themselves solely guilty in five of the eight charges.

In one charge (number 5) I find management guilty of viewing training as a reward and in one other (number 6) I hold both parties guilty of confusing 'reaction' with 'learning'. In charge number 4, I suspend judgment until training can prove that certain types of training do not provide learning.

On balance therefore, training will be sentenced to take remedial actions and to put their house in order.

My sentence is outlined in the next chapter.

CHAPTER 4

THE SENTENCE

I hereby sentence training to conduct meaningful training needs analyses using the Strategic Cascade.

If training is to be effective, it has to fit with what the organisation is trying to achieve in terms of its mission, strategies and objectives. As I pointed out in my verdict on several of the charges, trainers are often out of touch with the day to day needs of the organisation. Using the Strategic Cascade approach to TNA will help you to stop running meaningless courses and start suggesting some really useful performance improvement ideas!

THE STRATEGIC CASCADE

- Are mission and strategies clear?

- Are objectives being met?

- Is the culture congruent with the mission? (Do leaders 'walk the talk' and encourage employees to do so?)

- Are processes and structure geared to strategies and objectives?

- Do employees have the necessary knowledge, skills and attitudes to meet objectives?

TRAINING NEEDS ANALYSIS

The Strategic Cascade

1. Mission clear?	• Climate survey • Complaints • Interviews • 7 'S' analysis • Customer feedback • Union claims		Review long-term plans for impact on future mission and resulting training needs
		✗	Find out why
2. Objectives met?	• Analysis of key ratios • Participation in organisation performance reviews • Sales/productivity data • Benchmarking	✓	Anticipate future developments and training needs
		✗	Analyse reasons
3. Culture congruent with mission and objectives?	• Architecture/artifacts • Company reports & documentation • Reward system • Meeting behaviour • Climate survey		Monitor HR policy changes for effect on culture and future training needs
		✗	Identify sources of conflict
4. Structure and process geared to meet objectives?	• Benchmarking • Job descriptions • Customer/employees feedback	✓	Benchmark for developments in organisation design and implications for training needs
		✗	Analyse why structure or process is deficient
5. Individuals have knowledge, skills, attitudes necessary to meet objectives?	• Performance appraisal • Testing • Observation • Repertory grid • Questionnaires • Assessment centres		Monitor individuals' development plans for future training needs
			Establish reasons for the gap

Examples of Conclusions

- Senior management lack communication skills or awareness
- Middle management are blocking messages
- Culture does not favour disclosure

- Knowledge, skill or attitude gap
- Market/environmental conditions
- Force Majeure
- Critical incidents

- Rewarding A when hoping for B
- Managerial behaviour contradicts values
- Physical layout hinders communication

- Bad design
- Technology changed
- Customer or employee needs changed
- Lack of resources to update

- Age
- Motivation
- Lack of training

Examples of Action Ideas

- Provide top level coaching or communication training
- Conduct organisation development
- Implement culture change programme

- Define learning goals
- Design, develop and deliver training programmes to fill KSA gaps

---

- Recommend changes to reward system
- Use 360° instruments
- Conduct leadership seminars

- Propose training in new technologies
- Train in benchmarking if necessary
- Provide training in organisation theory

- Define learning goals
- Design, develop and deliver training

Most trainers seem to think that their job in analysing training needs starts by asking bosses and their teams what skills, knowledge and attitudes they need to do their jobs properly. This 'questionnaire' approach to needs analysis should be the **last** step!

An enormous amount of training fails because things in the organisation just aren't lined up in a way which will allow the right training to work for the right reasons.

1. Mission

As a trainer, the very first thing you must do if you want to do a useful TNA (Training Needs Analysis) is to find out:

• **Are the mission and strategies of the organisation clear?**

To do this you need to look at the various vision/mission/philosophy statements. You need to sit down with the key players and find out whether these statements tie in with where **they** think the organisation is going. Then ask whether people in the various teams reporting to them know about this overall direction and, indeed, whether they agree with it!
In some companies a lot of the employees think that the mission is just some silly soft stuff that a senior manager has copied from a book.

Now, at this stage, you don't need to investigate whether people actually 'walk the talk' and demonstrate that they act in accordance with the mission (that's for step 3). You just need to find out whether they know about it.

Here are some ways to find out:

- **Climate surveys** - just ask them! 'To what extent do you know ....?'
- **Feedback from customers** – do they indicate that your staff know about the mission and current strategies?
- **Interviews** – what do people tell you when you ask them to state the mission?
- **Union claims** – what does the feedback from employee representatives tell you?
- **Complaints** – usually indicating where performance deviates from the mission.
- **7 'S' analysis** – Bob Waterman's classic model for analysing organisations can be used to determine to what extent the mission has permeated through to the key organisational processes – (shared values, systems, strategy, structure, staff, style and skills).

If the evidence you collect tells you that the mission and strategies of the organisation are indeed clear, then you're off to a good start for providing training that will work. However, don't rest on your laurels – you should be looking at future changes in strategy (and they can happen overnight because of market or technology changes) to be ready with possible performance improvement solutions.

However, if the answer to the question is 'no' then you've got to find out why the message isn't getting through. Are middle managers blocking the information flow because they're scared of losing power? Do top management lack the key communication skills? Whatever the reason, your job as a trainer is to help get this information down through the organisation. This may, in fact, mean providing training for the top executives in how to communicate, but more often than not it will mean:

- Helping the CEO to re-jig the mission statement so that it makes sense to everyone
- Designing and helping to conduct 'vision and values' discussions at all levels of the organisation, where people get the opportunity to talk about aligning their own values with those in the mission statement
- Helping to design/redesign publications (both internal and external) which communicate the mission and strategies to **all** the various stakeholders of the organisation

2. Objectives

As soon as you are satisfied that the organisation's mission and strategies are clear to the employees, you can move on to the second step in your TNA and ask:

- **Are the organisation's objectives being met?**

It may sound strange to some of you, but I find that many trainers operate in an organisational vacuum – creating and running training courses for employees in a kind of philanthropic daydream. They seem to believe that training is an acquired right, or sometimes even a welcome and necessary palliative to daily stress and injustice. It's as if they're working against the company instead of being constantly in touch with the nerve centre of objectives and performance, as they obviously should be.

So, trainers should be looking at:
- **Key ratios** – which financial/performance ratios are most significant in your business? How are you doing?
- **Sales/Productivity data** – what are the trends? What processes/steps need to be streamlined?
- **Benchmarking** – how do you compare with the best in your field?

You should also be participating in regular organisational performance reviews.

What? Neither you nor your boss is invited to attend these meetings? You are not on the circulation list for performance data?
Maybe this partly accounts for my verdict against you!

If, on the other hand, you are in the performance review loop and all the major organisational objectives are being met, then think ahead and look at the five year plan. What future objectives are likely to put a strain on people's ability to perform as well as they do today?

If objectives are not being met, then you'll need to analyse why. In many cases the reasons have nothing to do with training. Market conditions may have been such that sales quotas could not be met. Maybe a decision by major stakeholders forced management to change their priorities.

In some cases there are gaps and deficiencies in people's knowledge, skills and attitudes which cause them to miss their objectives. This is where you can propose specific training interventions, the impact of which can be measured.

3. Culture

Thirdly, and perhaps most importantly, trainers should be asking:

- **Is the culture congruent with the mission?** (Do leaders 'walk the talk' and encourage employees to do so?)

One of the most frustrating things about designing and delivering training is that some organisations reward A while hoping for B! In other words, they keep paying bonuses for certain results (like short-term sales volume or cost cutting) while hoping that some 'invisible hand' will lead them to live by the mission statement which calls for things like 'long-term thinking' or 'investing in growth'.

CEOs and leaders will often ask you to provide training, but fail to realise to what extent the organisation may actually discourage people from using what they have learned. For example, I've heard of managers, returning from a creativity course, being told by their boss to stick to methods which work ('look what happened to the last guy who tried doing things in a new way!'). Is your organisation hoping for a certain kind of new behaviour but supporting a culture which rewards something else? If it is, then you'll probably find that even the best designed and conducted training courses will be a waste of time and money.

Here are some of the questions you should be asking and answering before embarking on an expensive but useless training adventure:

- **Architecture/artifacts** – does the layout, design, size and decoration of offices fit with what the mission/charter says about how people should be treated? What about the car park? (Free for all or privileged spaces?) What about perks for certain positions, status symbols, etc?

- **Company documentation** – what image do internal/external company publications convey compared with values expressed in the mission?

- **Reward system** – what behaviour does the organisation's pay and bonus system reward? Is this congruent with what the mission says the organisation believes in?

- **Meeting behaviour** – do meetings reflect the kind of values stated in the mission?

Continued over ...

- **Climate survey** – what do employees say about managers 'walking the talk'?

- **Management behaviour** – what have you observed when it comes to managers practising what the mission preaches?

If the answer to any of these questions leads you to suspect that culture and mission are not congruent, then training probably won't work. It could even be counter-productive in that it could awaken expectations and create frustrations. In this case, you have some serious organisation development work to do, starting with a visit to top management to explain your misgivings.

And, even if today's culture is congruent with today's mission, think ahead. In this ever-changing world there'll be all sorts of possible cultural pitfalls. Your job is to identify them and highlight them to management to avoid wasting money on useless training.

4. Structure and process

Fourthly, you should seriously analyse whether the organisation and structure of your company are appropriate for its present needs by asking:

- **Are structures and processes geared to strategies and objectives?**

It is difficult for people to function properly if the organisation is not structured properly, or if the process of doing business is outdated or if the technology lags behind. In these situations a training need is often wrongly identified because some vital structural alteration has been deferred or is not recognised at all. If this is the case there is very little likelihood that performance will improve, and staff become very cynical about such exercises. For example, there's no point in training people in how to communicate well with customers if the computer system which deals with their orders is inadequate.

The organisation needs to be constantly changing in line with environmental conditions. You can usually find out quite easily to what extent systems are in sync with objectives by asking the following questions:

- **Benchmarking** - how do others in our field do it?
- **Job descriptions** - are they relevant, adhered to, stagnating?
- **Customer feedback** - are processes designed to suit you or the customer?
- **Employee feedback** - ask them if they know a better way.
- **Re-engineering** - would you do it exactly the same if you were to start over?
- **Competencies** - are they linked to strategic objectives?

Some organisations waste resources on training which has little effect on organisational performance. The analysis above may lead you to conclude that bad design, technology, or a poor process is behind the dip in effectiveness.

If this is the case, your job is then to report back to management so that the processes, systems or structures can be updated **before** you waste your precious training resources on useless courses.

5. Knowledge, skills and attitudes

Lastly, I sentence you to do last what most trainers do first, namely to ask:

- **Do employees have the necessary knowledge, skills and attitudes to meet objectives?**

Having gone through the cascade, and having exhausted the alternative explanations for the performance problems, you are left with the distinct possibility that there may be a lack of knowledge, skills or attitude on the part of individuals. You can research this information through the following:

- **Performance appraisal** - what does the system tell us?
- **Testing** - what can people do?
- **Observation** - what does the boss think?
- **Repertory grid** - what do staff need to do to be successful?
- **Questionnaires** - what do they know?
- **Assessment centres** - what development needs do they have?

The answer to all these questions will provide you with the raw material for designing meaningful training courses – as long as all the other levels of the Strategic Cascade have been visited.

Failure to do so will result in retrial.

I should not need to point out that being found guilty a second time could well result in capital punishment – in other words the death of the training profession as we know it!

In addition, I sentence you to manage the Training Transfer Environment. This is a very complex process which I have summarised by calling it the 8 Ps - the Learning Transfer Bridge.

It seems to me that what you trainers are doing at the moment is taking participants through courses, seminars and workshops and leading them to the edge of u wide river. The other side of this river represents organisational performance improvement. At the end of the learning experience you push them into the river and tell them to swim to the other side.

No wonder so few of them make it! Some can't swim, others are swept away by the current. Those who finally make it are so exhausted that they have no strength left to change anything.

THE 8 Ps

With the 8 Ps, or the Learning Transfer Bridge, you'll be able to minimise all those forces that presently militate against getting results from training!

THE 8 Ps - THE LEARNING TRANSFER BRIDGE

1) Performance improvement plan

Establish overall training needs for individuals based on the cascade results and discuss/set expected outcomes.

2) Participation of line management in course design and delivery

Ensure that all courses are relevant, realistic and include 'transferability'.

3) Pre-course briefings

Set specific expectations and objectives for transfer of course learning back to the job and show linkages between using skills and job performance.

4) Preparation of learning log

Help participants to chart their progress towards behaviour change on a learning log.

5) **P**rogramme support

Restructure workload during and after programme to allow transfer of learning. Encourage a course environment where people can concentrate on learning.

6) **P**ost-course briefings

Finalise a plan for the transfer of learning to the job. Provide resources and give time for trying new skills.

7) **P**eer and team member support

Encourage use of knowledge, skills and attitudes by, for example, allowing participants to pass on training to colleagues and staff.

8) **P**rizes and sanctions

Reward people for transforming training into performance improvement.

1.
Performance improvement plan

If an organisation really wants to atone for the great training robbery, then it must have a performance improvement culture. Human performance improvement starts with a plan. Trainers should therefore be responsible for ensuring that every individual has an opportunity, at least once a year, to talk to their boss about how to do things better. The results of this discussion should be recorded on a Performance Improvement Plan (PIP).

Keep the PIP simple but include the following:

◆ **Link**
   How does this person's performance link with and contribute to the overall performance of the organisation.

◆ **Gap**
   What is the gap between the person's present performance and the organisation's expectations? How was this gap measured?

◆ Solutions

What training does the person need to bring about improved performance?
What other development activities should be planned? (job rotation, promotion, etc)
What other non training actions will/might help? (salary, job enrichment, process change, etc)

◆ Resources needed

What are the costs of these actions in terms of money, equipment, personnel, etc?

◆ Obstacles

Be realistic. What things will be hindering the achievement of the plan? (environment, culture, motivation of others, etc)

◆ Measurement

Finally, how will improvement be measured and rewarded? (objectives, follow-up, etc)

2.
Participation of line management in course design and delivery

One of the reasons that trainers have been robbed of their impact is that their well-meaning, beautifully designed courses are often not relevant, realistic or transferable. In other words, they are fabulous learning experiences in a watertight kind of way, but don't actually address the real performance gaps identified by their bosses.

Even if it **sounds** less professional, one way of overcoming this problem is to involve managers in course design and delivery. How can trainers make this happen without losing control of training quality?

Training Design and Delivery

◆ Get managers to 'sign off' on the learning objectives which are given to the course designers who will create the learning event.

◆ Get course designers and trainers to write down how the learning process, in the courses they are designing, will deliver what managers expect.

- Train managers to contribute at least one module to each course. OK, so they're not very professional trainers. Limit the potential disaster by providing **your** exercises or 'topping and tailing' the sessions with your own input. Even if managers are not as good as you at giving punchy training messages, the results will at least be linked to what they really want and need – and therefore to what they will measure and reward.

- If this is not realistic in terms of the managers' skills and/or availability, ask them (cajole, coax, blackmail) to **at least** open and close training events. This will lend credibility and impact to the training as will impromptu, interested visits by managers to training courses. Apart from anything else, this involvement keeps managers in tune with what training is trying to do to help **them** help their people improve.

3. Pre-course briefings

The transfer of learning must be managed.

This is one of the most vital steps in making sure that learning is transferred into performance improvement. Honestly speaking, how many participants on training courses have had briefing sessions with their bosses before they come? How many have discussed their mutual expectations as to what they will learn, and how they will put the learning into practice back on the job?

Your job as a trainer is to make sure these briefings take place. It's the old story, isn't it? Unless someone knows what is expected of them how on earth will they know if they have achieved anything?

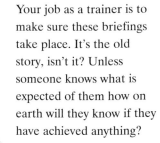

12.01.2001. 17 : 04
Brief 10.00 am
manager's office

The best way to conduct a pre-course briefing is to use the PIP (Performance Improvement Plan) or to refer back to the most recent appraisal discussion and to define some key learning objectives for the course. Help managers to set clear targets and insist that they agree on a date for a post-course briefing.

At this stage, learning objectives might sound like this:

At the end of this course the trainee will:
- ◆ Be able to use the new XYZ software
- ◆ Have learned and practised new presentation techniques
- ◆ Have acquired the knowledge about new EU regulations needed to modify procedures ABC
- ◆ Be able to explain the new mission and values statement to the team
- ◆ Know they have practised the steps involved in a good selection interview

Maybe you trainers should insist upon signed evidence that a pre-course briefing has taken place before you allow anyone to attend a course!

Sometimes, by making something more difficult to have, you make it more desirable.

4. Preparation of a learning log

As a professional trainer, you should be designing and distributing learning logs to all employees.

A learning log is essentially a notebook which will help trainees and their bosses make sure that the learning that takes place on training programmes, or during other development opportunities, is integrated into the day to day life of the organisation.

For each course or development opportunity a learning log might look like this:

COURSE LEARNING LOG

a. Expectations of participant:
What is s/he expected to achieve/do before, during and after the training?

b. Manager's role
How will s/he provide support?

c. Trainer's role
How can the trainer help the participant most?

d. Learning objectives
Make them measurable!

e. Learning achievements
What was actually learned? Proof?

f. Notes on post-course briefing
Details of the discussion/any action agreed

g. Action plans
Objectives to achieve as a result of learning

h. Obstacles to achieving objectives
Things/people/environmental considerations that could be working against achieving these objectives

i. Plans to overcome obstacles
How can boss/peers/colleagues help?

5. Programme support

There is no doubt that current training lowers current productivity. People can't attend courses **and** do their jobs at 100% efficiency. Nor should they be expected to get back to 100% immediately after a course – they should have time to practise the new learning.

Once you managers and trainers have understood this, then you can arrange temporary restructuring of the job to allow trainees to organise coverage of their job **before** the course, concentrate on learning **during** the course, and have some down-time to try out new skills and techniques **after** the course.

This is not easy because it often means a change of attitude from both manager and trainee. In some cases it also means a change in the culture of the organisation from 'training as a perk' to 'training as a vital investment for growth'.

What does programme support mean in terms of specific actions?

Before a Learning Event

Trainers should be coaching managers on how to create an environment where people like learning. Managers should start by setting a good example, by being 'learning individuals' themselves. Just as with learning organisations, managers need to encourage learning every day – in meetings, discussions, appraisals. Learning individuals do this by asking questions, reviewing PIPs regularly, commenting on their own learning, etc. On the practical side, both manager and trainee should be planning how to cover the trainee's job during the learning event to avoid stress and worry.

During the Learning Event

Above all, the boss should leave the trainee in peace during the training! No phone calls for information. No frantic e-mails demanding attention. On the contrary, maybe even a note or call of encouragement during the week. Even better (if feasible), a lightning visit to the training course for a chat on how it's going.

After the Learning Event

Because most people these days are overloaded with work, they have to put off practising new skills and techniques until that magic day when they will suddenly have time. What managers and trainers need to do is to recognise that the implementation of learning will require that some tasks be allocated to other team members (or quite simply postponed) so that the trainee can concentrate on trying out the new skills.

6. Post-course briefing

All the research data on transfer of learning says 'the longer you wait, the less you will use it'.

So, the first few days following a learning event are a vital time. In fact, it seems to me that steps 6 and 8 in the 8 Ps represent the key to the success or failure of training programmes. My research shows me that very few organisations are systematically conducting post-course briefings. No wonder training is robbing the organisation of its resources – but then managers are also guilty of wasting the investment.

If trainers **and** managers showed some common sense and insisted on using a learning log to conduct post-course objective setting sessions and then rewarded people for achieving those objectives, I would be satisfied that the sentence had succeeded in purging the crime.

Specifically this means:
- Turning the pre-course learning objectives into performance objectives
- Identifying obstacles to achieving these objectives (plans to overcome the obstacles will be covered in step 7)

So, taking those examples of learning objectives I gave in the pre-course briefing, the learning log might look like this:

Action Plans
- All sales reports will be produced on XYZ software by year end
- My next three presentations will have been structured using the newly learned model and the feedback sheet I distribute will show a score of over 3 out of 5 for 'body language'
- By end July our ABC procedures will have been rewritten in line with new EU legislation
- I will have conducted two 'mission and values' meetings with my team and obtained an 80% commitment to the statement
- By October 31, an observer will have confirmed that at least two selection interviews that I conducted followed the steps learned

Obstacles to Achieving Objectives
- Time/opportunity to practise
- Acceptability of feedback sheet to audience
- Acceptability to team members of 'being told values'

7. Peer and team support

From my own experience of training courses, I remember how difficult it was for me as a young lawyer to practise what I had learned. In fact, in some cases I was positively discouraged by the senior partner who considered I'd been on a vacation, or by colleagues who thought I was rocking the boat.

So I sympathise with you trainers and managers. But that doesn't diminish your responsibility!
Do as I say; not as I did!

Seriously though, to overcome those obstacles you've identified on the learning log, bosses have to take a team approach. One way of encouraging peer and team support is to organise *sharing sessions* when a team member returns from a learning event. The trainee presents the key learning points and discusses the relevance of this learning to the job with colleagues. Again, the learning log can be used to jot down agreements on the support which each colleague will provide.

The manager's role in restructuring the trainee's workload is vital here. People need time and space to practise.

Managers might also be encouraged to provide support by establishing *learning pairs* within the team.
A learning pair is simply two people who have attended the same training event. Their job as a pair is to compare notes on the effectiveness of the training they received and to support each other in putting the learning to work.

8. Prizes and sanctions

In most of the organisations I have come across, people tend to do what they are paid to do. They concentrate on the priorities set by their boss. As healthy human beings they naturally seek rewards rather than punishment.

In my view, the fundamental reason for the Great Training Robbery is that most of the time, in most organisations, most people are not rewarded for putting into practice what they learned in training. On the contrary, they're sometimes actually punished for trying to ('Enjoyed holiday? Now – back to the real world,' 'Don't rock the boat,' 'We're not having any of that 'touchy-feely' stuff in this department, I can tell you,' 'We'd love to use these new systems but we simply can't afford the equipment needed!').

Quite frankly, trainers who cannot influence their organisations to reward new behaviours will soon be up in court again accused of squandering resources.

Just imagine how much more seriously training would be taken if people's salaries (or even just their bonuses) were totally dependent on them putting into practice what they learned on courses!

Without going that far, prizes for new behaviours come in many forms:

◆ Salary increases
◆ Bonus payments
◆ Praise and recognition
◆ New and more interesting projects
◆ Higher quality of working life

Please note that this last part of your sentence is by no means optional. Without reward, behaviour won't change. Without behaviour change, training is a waste of time and money.

You have been warned! Remember what I said about trainers being found guilty a second time (page 71).

JOHN AND PAUL'S CONCLUSION

Well, there you have it.

Training was found guilty on six of the eight charges that they themselves brought against management!

The sentence sounds simple – take the Strategic Cascade approach to training needs analysis and help the organisation manage the transfer environment with the 8 Ps.

However, this may mean a radical change in the way trainers **and** their organisations view training.

Too much to ask?

Well, don't blame us if, next time, training is accused of being the sole perpetrator of the Great Training Robbery!

About the Authors

John Townsend has spent over 30 years fighting the fraud!
He holds a BA in Social Psychology from Exeter University in the UK and an MA in Human Resource Development from Webster University in the USA. He is a member of ASTD and of the Chartered Institute of Personnel & Development.
John has worked in senior human resource management positions in the UK, France, Switzerland and the USA and spent 15 years as Training Director with GTE where he was responsible for the competency development of thousands of managers and professionals. In 1996, after 12 years as an independent leadership training consultant, John founded the Master Trainer Institute, a unique train-the-trainer facility near Geneva, Switzerland.

John is the author of several best-selling management books including The Trainer's Pocketbook and (with Paul Donovan) The Facilitator's Pocketbook, and his Video Arts CD/video packages are now bringing his powerful messages into management training courses all over the world.

Contact
You can visit John's Master Trainer Institute web site on:
http://www.mt-institute.com
Alternatively, contact him at:
The Master Trainer Institute,
L'Avant Centre, 13 chemin du Levant,
Ferney-Voltaire, France.
Tel: (+33) 450 42 84 16   Fax: (+33) 450 40 57 37
E-mail: john.townsend@wanadoo.fr

Paul Donovan MSc (Mgmt.)

Paul is Senior Programme Director with the Irish Management Institute in Dublin where he is responsible for a suite of training and development programmes for HRD professionals.

He has extensive management experience and has conducted a wide range of HRD assignments in Western Europe and Asia.

Paul's professional interests include researching evaluation of training and development interventions where he has identified easy-to-use surrogate measures as effective replacements for time consuming and expensive evaluation initiatives. He has edited seven books in a series of management texts and is co-author of The Facilitator's Pocketbook.

Contact

Paul Donovan can be contacted at:
Irish Management Institute,
Sandyford,
Dublin 16
Ireland.
Tel: (+353) 1 2078474
E-mail: donovanp@imi.ie

The Great Training Robbery
is one of four titles in a
series of Pocketbook
Squares, retailing at £9.99

The other titles are:
Hook Your Audience, Leadership: Sharing the Passion
and **The Great Presentation Scandal.**

Other titles in the Pocketbook series include:

The Trainer's Pocketbook, The Trainer Standards Pocketbook, The Challengers Pocketbook and (illustrated) **The Facilitator's Pocketbook.**

The Management Pocketbook Series

Order Form

Your details

Name

Position

Company

Address

Telephone

Facsimile

E-mail

VAT No.
(EC companies)

Your
Order Ref

Please send me:

No. copies ▼

The Great Training Robbery

The   Pocketbook

The   Pocketbook

The   Pocketbook

The   Pocketbook

Order by Post

Management Pocketbooks Ltd
14 East Street, Alresford, Hampshire SO24 9EE UK

Order by Phone, Fax or Internet

Tel: +44 (0)1962 735573
Fax: +44 (0)1962 733637
E-mail: sales@pocketbook.co.uk
Web: www.pocketbook.co.uk

MANAGEMENT POCKETBOOKS

Customers in USA should contact:

Stylus Publishing, LLC
22883 Quicksilver Drive, Sterling, VA 20166-2012
Telephone: 703 661 1581 or 800 232 0223
Facsimile: 703 661 1501 E-mail: styluspub@aol.com